EMPOWERED THROUGH

REAL ESTATE

21 Real Estate Business Ideas

How to Make Money in Real Estate without a License

CATINA R. WILLIS, MBA

Real Estate Broker - Investor - Online Business Coach

ISBN: 978-1-7350602-6-2

Real Estate: Entrepreneurship

In an effort to support local single mothers in urban areas, a portion of the book proceeds will be donated to Next Level Detroit, a nonprofit organization 501c3. Visit NextLevelDetroit.org for more information.

For discounted bulk orders of this book,
please call (734) 506-0076 ext. 1.

CONTENTS

DEDICATION

Congratulations on taking the first step in exploring the possibility of starting a real estate business. Many think of real estate and think "I don't want to be a REALTOR showing houses for people to say "nah, I don't like that one." This book will reveal the many levels of real estate businesses including property management companies, real estate investing, veteran homes, short term rentals (also known as Airbnb), the list could go on and on. I really put my heart and soul into this book during the initial stay home order for Covid-19. The information in this book is dedicated to people laid off from work. My goal for this book is to help someone start a successful business in the real estate industry during this uncertain time.

First, I would like to thank God for giving me strength, humility, a gift, and the perseverance to move forward with my personal dream of entrepreneurship. There were many unforeseen obstacles that were trying to stop me from completing this book. But, God has protected me during this life transition and connected me with the right team to help showcase my vision and expand my organization. Next, I want to give a very special thanks to the featured business owners mentioned throughout the text. These individuals were kind enough to share their stories about starting their business. ***Damon Thompson, Deonte*** *and Devona Johnson, Emma Elder-Howell, Jay Barnes, Rochelle Nelson, and Tracey Spencer.* Learning about your extraordinary journeys gave this book, relatable examples of how to move forward successfully in such a competitive industry.

Now it's time to thank family. I'll just start off with the absolute best real estate assistant for a person like me. Thank you *Dominique Currie* for always being flexible, positive, and willing to help, no matter how big or small the task is. *TaNeal Green,* thank you for your support with proofreading of this book. Our reconnection during this process shows the importance of family bonds and ties.

Lastly, I want to dedicate this book to any women that are currently going through hardships or have been affected by domestic violence. I wrote this book with you in mind. A portion of the proceeds go to *Next Level Detroit,* a nonprofit 501c3 that I started in 2019. Initially, the purpose of this book was to raise funds for the organization. Our mission is to help provide affordable housing, support, and resources to women dealing with hardships. With women of color being the largest percentage of people renting and being evicted; we want to help bring pride and ownership back to urban neighborhoods. Next Level Detroit is governed by six chair members. I am the President and founder. Learn more about this organization by visiting *nextleveldetroit.org.*

As you begin reading this book, you will start to see just how powerful you can be with a real estate business. My company started out as a traditional real estate brokerage, just helping people buy and sell real estate. Today, I'm really changing lives and making a difference. We've blossomed into being a real estate resource for women of color. Our goal is to help revitalize the city one house at a time, by increasing homeownership through creative house buying programs. We want to give women dealing with hardships a different opportunity in this unfair game of Monopoly.

INTRODUCTION

As I grow through my real estate business experiencing highs and lows, the quarantine of Covid-19 forced me to sit still for a minute and reflect. I started to wonder what real estate would look like after a vaccine is created; I wondered if the real estate market would be up or down when this is over. I thought about a lot, including the times when I had the most success in my real estate business; and the times I struggled the most. When I was a new REALTOR, I didn't see many women who looked like me as leaders. There were no books or easy to find mentors to tell me the do's and don'ts of the industry. I had to research and seek information on my own. However, my determination and willingness to learn, helped me navigate through this field and grow into the business woman you see today; always taking chances and trying to move forward fearlessly. Starting a business is intimidating just like writing this book. You don't know what critics will say and again, there's really no pamphlet telling you how to avoid mistakes. This is why I am so passionate about sharing as many real estate business tips and practices that I can. I started sharing my real estate experiences a few years ago, through my book, blogs, and YouTube channel. My purpose was to make life a little easier for new real estate professionals and especially women of color in real estate. Believe it or not, minorities still face unfair challenges when working as a REALTOR; even if they have more education or experience. The small business grants and assistance for Covid-19 in urban areas are unequal as well. Covid-19 has caused massive lay-offs, job cuts, fear, and anxiety. Many workers are searching for something different to do for a living; including myself. The beginning of the pandemic had me reflecting on all the major life changing experiences I've encountered. During the 2008 mortgage crisis I was an inexperienced landlord and I've been reflecting back on what I learned during that era. When the market crashed, I was extremely concerned and afraid, just like most people. I thought my house would never be viewed as an asset again, and I'd be paying the mortgage forever with no equity. I knew I could not be still and wait for the crisis to overcome me; so I became proactive and started formulating a plan for my family. Learning how to navigate through uncertainty and push forward when there was no vision for the housing crisis took courage. Ultimately, I sought out programs to reduce the interest rate and monthly payment on my primary home; my investment properties were underwater, so I let many go. Later, after the storm calmed down a bit, I was able to start fresh and buy better cheaper properties. Call me crazy but I believe Covid19 will be a similar situation.

As you read this book I will explain how to brainstorm and create a business during this global uncertainty. The information shared in this book will divulge real estate as a potential exit strategy for employed and unemployed people. We must fight and not let a temporary displacement detour our business goals during job uncertainty and economic changes. 6 | Empowered through Real Estate

Back to the mortgage crisis in 2008 and 2009; I learned that bad times present new opportunities. After losing multiple houses during that time, I should have realized that it was a cleansing. It was time to buy new houses without mortgages. Like many, starting new in the real estate business, I wasn't wise enough to understand the shake-up that was taking place within the industry. That's when I should have tried to buy the block! Like in the famous board game Monopoly. You see, real estate is similar to stocks. What goes up, must come down and vice versa. The real estate market has a major shift every ten to twelve years. I understand this now but back in 2008, I thought the real estate game as I knew it WAS OVER!

What are my thoughts about businesses changing how they operate because of Covid-19? Sometimes change is good, and it is the time to reinvent ourselves. Unlike 2008, I'm much wiser now and understand the industry transformation this time. I'm already seeing opportunities that were not present last year or the last few years. Furthermore, launching any business today is much easier than it was a decade ago; mainly, because of social media. As you continue reading through the chapters, you will see exact social media marketing strategies that turned posts into dollars for a local Detroit small business owner.

"This book is designed to help people with business ideas to finally execute!"

Years from now, when you think of 2020, what will be the first thing that comes to mind? I ask this question because some people will remember 2020 as the year they lost a loved one. Some will think of 2020 as the year they leveled up in life financially. Finally, some people will remember 2020 as the year they reinvented themselves. One thing's for sure, about 2020, many people have more time, and some of us have adapted to change well, or leveled up in our field. Since my first book, I have been thinking about writing another. I was certain I'd write a book about investing in Detroit real estate. However, 2020 and Covid-19 was the perfect, most memorable time to write. As the world is changing and so many people are at home, it's the prime time to start thinking of ways to upgrade your economic situation. I know it's easier said than done especially with so many obstacles in the way and everything moving a lot slower than it used to. I'm not saying it will be easy, but baby steps will get you there. For instance, take the 45 minutes you use to spend in rush hour traffic traveling to work and meditate about your passions. Then keep a journal book to just write your ideas down. For me, 2020 will be the year I not only remember wearing a mask just to go into the store, but I'll remember it as the year I wrote and published a book to help people build a real estate business. I'll also remember 2020 as the year I got my family puppy. Another big event I'll remember is 2020 was the year I took my real estate business all the way to the next level. You see I got my Brokers license in 2015. A Broker is a real estate agent who can open a legal firm and put other real estate sales agents under the Broker. 2020 is the year I realized my company and brand needed more meaning.

I started to have a deep desire to do more than just help people buy and sell real estate. I wanted to solve problems that many were not concerned with. This is how Next Level Detroit, (a non-profit 501c3 organization) was born. My original plan was to start an all-women's organization that focused on providing housing to single women. Next Level Detroit has already grown, and we focus on building the self-esteem of women through real estate and financial literacy. Additionally, we provide affordable housing, resources, and support to single mothers. I want women to know they can evolve and get out of many situations with proper planning and coaching. With talks of a possible recession coming, and a big real estate shift; this time, I'll be prepared and can help prepare others. Knowledge is power and no one can take knowledge away. As you start reading the first chapter, ideas and execution strategies should immediately start growing in you. Go ahead and keep reading! Also, be sure to write your goals and thoughts after each chapter. This way you can reflect on your growth a year from now.

Most millionaires will tell you, if you don't write goals down, you're just dreaming.

CHAPTER 1

WHEN ONE DOOR CLOSES

You probably picked up this book for two reasons. First, your sense of job security has changed, or second, maybe you're just tired of working for someone else, and you're thinking, "What else can I do or how can I work for myself?" Ever hear the old saying "when one door closes, another door opens?" You've heard for years that people need multiple streams of income. However, you've never had the time to think of creating a side hustle or business. I wanted to be an entrepreneur my whole life but didn't really know how to get started. The desire got stronger as I entered my mid-thirties. I remember being at my job and thinking, I can do this better or I'm too smart to be sitting here 8 hours a day with someone giving me permission to take a day off. After finally getting the courage to resign from my job, I found myself stuck at first. Didn't really have a solid job lined up, just hopes of a part-time position as a professor, at a creative arts school. While I waited for the call, I started my first company called Supra Internet. Needless to say, it was a bust! The goal was to become a huge internet marketing company that offered graphic designs and social media promotions for small businesses. My passion must not have been strong enough because I stopped promoting the company within 30 days. Eventually, I did land the job working as an Adjunct Professor teaching Internet Marketing and Business courses. My excitement for that job was gone after the second semester. But during that time is when I got my real estate license. After a failed company and failed new career, I decided to put 110% of my energy into real estate and that's when the "New Me" was born. Continue reading this book to find out why many, maybe including you, procrastinate, or have the fear of leaving a job to launch something of your own. I do understand that entrepreneurship is not for everyone. However, I also understand everyone should be able to generate income from their GOD given talents or hobbies. It is my promise that when you complete this book and really absorb what our featured business owners share, you will have a desire to become a business owner or just an individual who can make a living without a traditional J. O. B. All I ask is that you don't become the person looking at everyone else wondering, "WOW, how did they do it?" Be the person everyone else is looking at and wondering how YOU did it!

Let me share my background with you. I spent 15 years as a salaried employee in the real estate field. In my last 4 years, I worked as a Marketing Coordinator. I have a bachelor's degree in marketing. Also, I earned a master's degree in business administration, during my time as an employee. Over the years, through trial and error, I've learned a lot about what it takes to start a business. I have also learned how to draw attention to the product or service of that business with Marketing and Promotions. Although I am proud of my education, I don't think degrees can make a person successful in business; talent, skills, consistency, and passion does! I learned that people don't get paid for degrees, but people get paid for the knowledge and skills they've mastered. I say this because after obtaining an MBA, I searched and searched for jobs that required this type of degree. But I wasn't getting callbacks from jobs that paid enough. I tried being an Adjunct professor for a while teaching business and marketing courses, but that didn't pay enough. Furthermore, I also failed with a few businesses and wanted to get my old job back several times. I say this to explain, the degrees didn't help me make a living doing something I'm obsessed with, I just discovered what I was good at and grew from it.

Since 2013, I've started multiple income-generating companies. Which include a property management company that was started in 2015. A consulting and coaching company that was created in 2017, a full-service real estate brokerage and investment firm which launched in 2018, and Next Level Detroit, (a nonprofit 501c3) which was founded in 2019. You can support the cause at **NextLevelDetroit.org**.

My entrepreneurial spirit formed when I worked as a marketing coordinator. I learned a lot about marketing, promotions, and launching new products. As I reflect back, this is why I'm able to think of new companies and execute quickly.

I learned about real estate investing after purchasing my first home in 2000. After the closing, my Realtor asked, "have you ever thought about buying investment properties to rent?" We thought about it for a few weeks, and late 2000 was when I first became a landlord. As you continue reading this book, you'll learn how one single investment house turned me into an entrepreneur on the rise. Now, some people may not consider a real estate investor or a real estate agent as an entrepreneur or small business owner; but the person most definitely is. I look at each house as a new project or a new business. Landlords and real estate investors develop a strategy for each house every time. It's not always buying and renting for $800 per month. They take calculated risks each time they invest funds into buying a house. They generate leads with marketing and convert leads into paying tenants.

When I launched my real estate sales business in January 2013, it was like my baby. Since then, I've built a database of more than 900 people and sold almost 1,000 residential and commercial properties. Now, keep in mind, that the average REALTOR sells about 6 to 12 properties each year. Also, many real estate brokerages don't hand over clients or pay REALTORS to work, we pay them!!! When a REALTOR is new, they usually sign up with big real estate companies to get guidance and learn the business. Most big companies usually provide training 4-5 days a week, costs are higher, and very few leads are usually provided by the company. Smaller companies like Next Level Realty & Investments usually have weekly training, lower costs, and daily leads provided. To learn more about my real estate brokerage, visit EmpoweredThroughRealEstate.com. Getting my real estate brokerage growing took lots of planning, studying, marketing, promotions, good customer service skills, following up, networking, more than $15,000 in courses, blood, sweat, and tears. Oh, and YES, I would do it all again. I went from being a lady with a JOB, to starting four businesses in 7 years! ALL 100% owned by a black woman. Just a girl from the eastside of Detroit who got kicked out of Denby high school and graduated from Finney after having to take a few freshman courses again senior year. I share my accomplishments, not to brag but as MOTIVATION!!!

Enough about me, the rest of this book is all about helping you make the decision to start generating income for yourself based on a gift you already have. Do you agree we all have special talents? Have you explored your talents? Do you think you can profit from your talents? These are questions you need to ask yourself if you plan to use your natural skill set to create another stream of income. I challenge you, to do a self-evaluation. This will help you consider your talent as a business. For example, maybe drawing is your gift. You can use your drawing skill as a way to generate income by designing T-shirts for a friend who is a REALTOR, or create real estate book covers. I understand most people are afraid at first to reveal their gifts to the world. However, whatever your favorite hobby or talent is, I challenge you to post a picture or video on social media. You might be surprised how many inquiries you'll get about it. BOOM! That could be the beginning of a small business.

After starting and launching Next Level Detroit, my nonprofit, it took me a few months to even speak about it. When I finally revealed and announced it, a donation was received within 24 hours. This donation was triggered by posting pictures of possible logos on Facebook. That's the power of social media. It's one of my favorite marketing tools. Continue reading as we will discuss social media in detail in a later chapter.

Now, we are about to get to the good part of this book. We have seven (8) featured business owners who were happy to share their journey. All of them were *Empowered through Real Estate* in some shape or form. I have interviewed each and every one of them to learn the highs and lows they have experienced over the years. They all agree that social media is a powerful tool for business owners to use in 2020.

Let me introduce Damon Thompson first. He decided to become a business owner after working in one of the most affluent suburbs outside of Detroit. His responsibility while working for this city was to get nonprofit organizations funded. As time went on, he noticed many of the organizations had a mission statement. In many cases, the mission statement said, they were helping people of color in the inner city. He later learned many of these organizations were not helping and were not really aware of the problems in urban areas. Many non-minorities were getting funded with grants for the inner city yet, they did not understand the issues that were happening in the inner city, nor were they actively serving people in the city. This caused him to take a step back, think, reflect, and launch his own organization. Damon started his business by conducting "How to Start a Non-Profit" classes in the basement of his church for FREE. Over the years he has built a portfolio of business and grant writing classes offered at a very affordable price. Damon used the knowledge he gained on the job to start his own business. Damon says **"if a man**

has a talent or learns something on the job, he should be able to use that skill for himself." Damon receives new clients through networking and word of mouth referrals.

Words of wisdom from Damon:

» Don't look for money. Do the work and the money will find you.

» Your talent and the relationships you have will generate income.

» Celebrate the baby steps and let go of fearing the unknown.

» If you have a 9 to 5, you could use the same energy to start your own business.

» Change your circle! Get around like-minded people who will push you to step outside your comfort zone.

You can find Damon on Facebook under Thompson Business Services, LLC. Or visit DTConsultBiz.com

THOMPSON
BUSINESS SERVICES, LLC
YOUR DREAMS + MY WORK = SUCCESS

You can't receive what you aren't prepared for

I saw a post on social media the other day stating, "Many people are really coming up as a result of a pandemic, what a shame," she said. Of course, I had to ask her if she was aware that many millionaires today increased their riches during a recession or bad times. This pandemic has shown me that tough times bring about different opportunities. Some people seek information or develop new skills during a downturn. Think about it, when has there ever been a time people could delay paying their rent, mortgage, or even credit cards? Less bills equal more money to invest or buy houses. Or maybe a reduced amount of bills help people to focus more on other things outside of their job. Regardless of why some people increase their riches during bad times, a person can't receive what they aren't prepared for. For instance, many employed people were upset that folks were getting paid hundreds of dollars a week to sit at home collecting unemployment funds. The people could not have received the money if they didn't have a job or work as an independent contractor. Some people were upset about folks getting hundreds of thousands of dollars in Covid business loans and grants. These people could not have received these funds if they did not start an LLC, and have an employer identification number (EIN) already. We will discuss in a later chapter how to start an LLC and obtain an EIN; this way you can be prepared in case other opportunities like these arise in the future. When I see people upset about another person's blessing, I want to say 'simmer down, you have no idea what they have gone through to be prepared for this.' Now let's move on to discovering your passions. Do you believe each and every person has something they are passionate about? When we truly find our passion, it feels good, it feels natural, and time flies quickly when we engage in it because we're having fun. So let's get a little interactive with this book; It's time for business brainstorming!

1. Grab a notebook just to write your ideas.
2. Find a quiet place in your home.
3. Dedicate 30 minutes a day to just think and write ideas.
4. Keep this notebook by your bedside; great ideas will come to you really late at night or early morning.
5. Grow and develop these ideas each day.

Thinking big and planning ahead can prepare anyone for workforce freedom. Brainstorming can broaden your mindset about how to start and grow any type of business. Now you might be thinking "everyone isn't meant to be an entrepreneur!" You're right! It's not easy either but the knowledge is good to have in case you experience employment issues in the future; so let's get to it.

Now let's take it back to the old days and memorize how people started businesses back then. I picture family and friends being excited and sampling the product or service. I can see the entrepreneur passing out flyers and knocking on doors with a sales pitch ready. These are techniques that still work today; I've personally used many to grow my business along with newer marketing techniques, like Facebook, Instagram, and YouTube. I can almost guarantee these new school marketing techniques are the most cost-efficient and time-effective strategies for any new business owner. Social media enables you to literally send a message to thousands of people with little time and money. Billions of people log into Facebook daily; and more than 40% log in to Facebook for news updates and referrals. So why not use it to share your talents and get clients?

It's time to confront your limiting beliefs

After reading my thoughts about sharing talents and gifts on social media, you might feel too shy to perform. Do you believe we are what we think and speak? Many confident people tell themselves daily that they can do something or they are something. They force themselves to actually become it. Our thoughts are so powerful! I'm challenging you to be like NIKE and JUST DO IT! If you draw, cook, run, create wigs, or build desks; post a picture or video on social media showing the world. Thinking and communicating to ourselves about what we CAN do, has a powerful, positive impact on us. When we tell ourselves we're not good enough or can't do something; the power of that negative thought will work against us. Remember, whatever you say about yourself prevents and tells the universe to give you and what your heart desires. So, what should you do when those negative thoughts come to you? Tell yourself that you can only think about or concentrate on one thing at a time. Then make a choice to be optimistic. If you find yourself thinking, "I could never start a business, I don't have this or that," offer an immediate rebuttal, such as, "I can do it if I learn the business and put in the same hours I did learning my current job." Prove it to yourself by taking one step at a time. Don't try to overthink it. Take the first step by getting a journal book and writing a promise letter to yourself. Give yourself an end goal date to have a business idea and business name chosen. I trust that as you continue reading this book, you will find your passion, you don't need me to cheer you on about it.

EMPOWERMENT PLAN

1. **Make a Decision**: Spend some quiet time with yourself. No kids, no spouse, just you, and your higher power. Talk, pray, meditate. Decide you will work on yourself for one hour per day. Create a new space in your home for quiet time and organizing your thoughts. Tell the family when you go there, they should not interrupt. Discuss what you're doing with your family, so they fully support your decision to do something that will help improve your lives.

2. **Write and say affirmations to yourself throughout the day**. Empower yourself by looking in the mirror and saying "I am skilled", I can do anything I put my mind to, I am courageous, my soul attracts the most talented

people, I am blessed with amazing friends and family. You get the point. So make your own affirmations and start shifting the way you think of your powers. Make a new routine to talk to yourself about how powerful, happy, beautiful, and motivated you are. People often ask how I stay smiling and appear so happy all the time. I believe it's because I made a decision to be happy. Also, I am always chasing attainable goals that give me fulfillment.

3. **Set Goals**. Get a notebook for documenting your goals and business ideas. Brainstorm and write down as many ideas as possible. Also, don't throw any paper away; some ideas may not make sense at first; however, it could pop up later as the missing piece of the puzzle. When you set goals and accomplish them, it sets the tone about who you are and it shows your level of determination. For example, I use to have a professional goal to write twelve contracts each month for my real estate business. Each month, when I reached the goals, it built my confidence to want to set the bar higher. One of my favorite quotes is *"If you don't set goals, life will be all about your problems."*

WRITE GOALS OR THOUGHTS HERE

_____

_____

_____

_____

_____

_____

_____

_____

_____

_____

_____

_____

_____

_____

_____

_____

_____

_____

_____

_____

_____

_____

_____

_____

_____

Chapter 2

The Lazy Landlord

W hen you think of real estate investing, what's the first strategy you learned? LANDLORDING! I can't tell you how many of my friends have grandmothers or grandfathers who owned houses and would visit the tenant each month to collect the rent. The tenant/landlord topic is the only real estate strategy some people know of; at least it was for me for many years. When I was a child, my grandmother owned the two-family flat that we lived in and a few others. My older brother Chico was responsible for cutting the grass at these properties. What I remember vividly was that my grandmother thought land lording was a headache. Many years later in my adulthood, I had heard so many horror stories about land lording and I later experienced some myself. Today I think land lording is extremely lucrative for some people but not ALL people. But why not all? Continue reading and you'll find out.

My insight into real estate investing has deepened over the years. I've made many mistakes as a young adult investing, and many more mistakes operating a property management company to help others. Additionally, as an agent, I've heard heartbreaking stories on landlording gone wrong and I'll always remember my grandmother's woes. This is probably the reason I don't have a large portfolio of houses; a few is good enough at this moment. I first got my feet wet in land lording in 2001 and the experience was bittersweet. Without going into too much detail, the tenant was a young, single woman with 3 children and we wanted to help her. We got the house approved for her section 8 voucher and she moved in soon after. Everything was going great, funds got deposited each month, on time, and we would make repairs whenever she called. Three years went by and the tenant had 2 more children. The house was at 18920 Hickory St. on the eastside of Detroit. See picture below courtesy of Realcomp.

It was an aluminum sided house featuring a living room, large updated eat-in kitchen, three bedrooms, one updated bathroom, and a crawl space. Only 971 square feet! There were now 6 people living in this house which caused me to be concerned. I personally don't think the space was adequate for a family that size. However, fair housing considers it discrimination to deny someone housing based on their family size. We continued receiving payments on time every month, which was the reason we turned the cheek and ignored her growing family. After the last maintenance repair, approximately six months went by and I noticed we hadn't heard from the tenant at all and her phone number was no longer in service. We used to drive by the house often the first year. It had been a while since we'd done that. One day we finally decided to drive by to check on the tenant and noticed that the house was completely abandoned. We asked a few neighbors who told us she moved out months ago. They said some people who looked like drug boys were there shortly after she left. Neighbors said they were in and out all the time. We went inside to inspect the house. Low and behold, the house was infested with mice and the completely remodeled house before the tenant moved in was now destroyed and in need of complete renovation. Can you imagine how upset we were? We thought this house would get us on the path to financial freedom but it's setting us back. This story is not meant to deter you against the idea of becoming a landlord. Just want to reveal my mistakes and the trials I experienced that makes me wiser today. As I mentioned earlier, landlording works out well for some. Just like with anything else, what you put into it is what you'll get out of it. Hickory was my first rodeo with landlording. Where did I go wrong? I failed to do routine interior inspections. I failed to thoroughly screen the tenant, and I'm sure we failed to do many other things successful landlords do, but this is how I learned.

Let's look at the numbers

The property was purchased for $18,000 with a hard money loan and refinanced shortly after. The monthly loan payment was approximately $448 and the tenant voucher paid $850 a month. After taxes and insurance, cash flow was $402 per month. That is how I invested in 2001.

Let's look at who you should be networking with as a landlord

- » Plumbers
- » HVAC (heating and cooling repair).
- » Handyman (routine maintenance man).
- » Painters
- » Electricians

Speaking of electricians and the people landlords should be networking with makes me think of Jay Barnes. People on Facebook call him Dr. Electrical or Dr. Good Energy.

Jay started his business after getting tired of working on a construction site. He quickly realized that getting a gig or contract/ job was extremely political. Most people in charge would select their friends and family for work, opposed to choosing the most skilled worker. Jay played politics for a while but one day he decided to take charge of his financial future by networking and gaining side jobs for homeowners. One day, (out of the blue) he was contacted by a property management company. The owner called him and the conversation went something like this, "Hi Jay, I'm a property manager and I've heard about your work. I recently fired my old electrician, can you do some electrical jobs for us?" Well, the rest is history. Jay is one of the most recommended electricians I've seen on social media. If anyone asks for an electrician he's tagged and recommended multiple times.

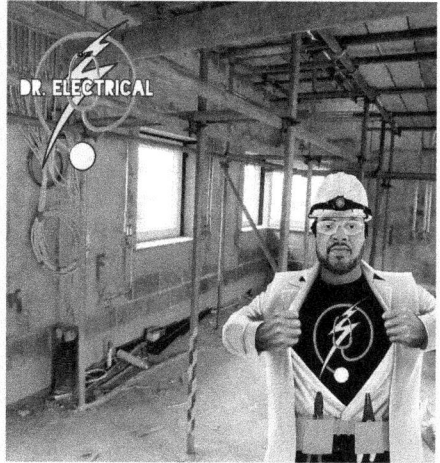

Jay says the key to really growing a business is being kind and consistent.

Jay recently launched a second business and he gives credit to social media for the fast growth. His second business is completely different from real estate. Jay once weighed 300 pounds. After he saw a picture of himself taken on his birthday, he decided to get in shape and start eating differently. He started following Dr. Sebi and learned about sea moss. On his weight loss journey, he would post pictures of his sea moss smoothies. Though he lost 75 pounds, something more magical happened, while Jay was getting fit. People started asking him if he sold sea moss smoothies. Originally he gave smoothies to 10 people for free. However, afterwards, he started selling the smoothies. Since Covid-19, people desire to get more vitamins and minerals in their bodies. As a result, his business has skyrocketed.

Jay tripled his income when he started working for himself. He used Facebook as his marketing strategy and didn't even have a formula. Jay says an online presence goes a long way. If people like you as a person, when you start selling something, some will personally advertise for you free of charge.

He made posts in all his Facebook groups with his company name, service offerings, and phone number. At first, it was just homeowner clientele, but he gradually got connected to REALTOR and Property Managers as clients.

Connect with Dr. Electrical on Facebook by searching Jay Barnes.

Here are 5 Strategies Skilled Landlords Follow

1. Inspect the property regularly! Tenants won't always bring maintenance repair issues to a landlord's attention. Mainly because they don't want the landlord all up in their business. It might make sense to have a plumber or HVAC guy visit the house yearly for routine maintenance. Remember, if a tenant does not own the house, they aren't considering the fact that a small minor issue can turn into a big expensive problem if ignored too long.

2. Screen tenants every time! Most first-time landlords choose the first person who has the funds to move into the property. I want you to remember this. It is easy to let someone move into your house, and it can be hell to get them out. With that being said, be sure to verify the tenant's employment history, references, credit, criminal background, all of that. Now you're probably thinking, "If they had perfect credit, they

would probably be buying a house." The credit check isn't to look for a perfect 700 or better score. It is to understand patterns and behavior. You can have them provide a recent credit report from myfico.com, or you can Google companies for landlords. Companies like Mr. Landlord will provide a credit report, and criminal history checks for less than $30.00. Additionally, always get a copy of the driver's license and social security card of all adults living in the house.

3. Walking through the property with the tenant. A move-in checklist will help the tenant understand your expectations for the property condition. Also, you can discuss the importance of reporting maintenance repairs as soon as the problem arises. Finally, have the tenant sign your move-in checklist.

I've learned many effective strategies that good landlords follow as a result of being the lazy landlord in the past. There aren't many people you'll talk to who don't have an interesting story to share about landlording or can't tell you the mistakes they made. One thing's for sure, owning properties can open a lot of doors and open your mind when done the right way. The purchase of just one house can lead to refinancing to get cash to buy 2 more. Or it can lead to buying a multi-family or apartment building. Once your brain expands, it can only continue to grow to bigger levels. I also previously discussed how landlording is the only investing business most people know of. Continue reading and you'll learn about real estate investing with no money or credit, the fix and flip business, also, adult foster care homes and short-term rentals. The sky is the limit when you're empowered through real estate.

EMPOWERMENT PLAN

1. Join investment groups in your area and on Facebook. You'll be able to connect with lenders who can help you finance investment properties. Also, find hard money and private lenders who loan money to buy rental properties.

2. Attend free seminars in your area OR online to learn about investing. You don't have to purchase anything. Just go for the freebies until you get a good understanding. There will be plenty of people to network with.

3. Consider buying a multi-family property with financing. You can live in one unit and rent the other. It's almost like living for free.

4. Find a good REALTOR and buy your first property. Search for a real estate agent who sells the type of property you want to buy. They are likely to have more expertise and resources for you.

5. Promote your properties through networks. Instead of traditional methods for spreading the "tenant wanted" message such as ads and signs. Try employer bulletin boards, networking, and referrals. You can also use an ad network that allows you to target prospective tenants based on where they play, work, or worship. Your advertisement should contain three main elements.

» A simple but attention-grabbing headline.
» List of benefits to the property renter.
» A call to action (call within 48 hours for a $25 discount on move-in costs).

Select your first tenant and sign the lease! Be sure to record a video of the property condition on the tenant's move-in day. Your next goal is to retain the tenant for as long as possible to reduce money spent renovating again.

WRITE GOALS OR THOUGHTS HERE

_____

_____

_____

_____

_____

_____

_____

_____

_____

_____

_____

_____

_____

_____

_____

_____

_____

_____

_____

_____

_____

_____

_____

_____

_____

_____

_____

_____

CHAPTER 3

OTHER PEOPLE'S HOUSES

Y ou've heard of using "Other People's Money" to invest in real estate. What about taking care of "Other People's Houses" who are investing in real estate? Why would anyone want to take annoying tenant repair calls, at all hours of the night for someone else? How about spending a few hours a day visiting the city about property certifications for someone else? Performing these tasks for someone else may not make a lot of sense at first; but it is what we call Property Management and it can be BIG Business. A property manager acts in the owner's absence and is the process of collecting rent, handling repairs and routine maintenance, screening tenants, getting city certifications and so much more. The city of Detroit is one of the most desired places for foreign investors because of the high return on investment. This is the reason Detroit property managers are in high demand! Landlording for other people has the potential to be extremely profitable with the right systems in place. Let's just say you're favorite REALTOR finds a great deal. It's a 3-bedroom brick house in a decent area and the price is $35,000. The rent is $800 per month. You're rental income will be $9,600 per year and after taxes and maintenance, your cash flow $6,192. That's an 18% return on investment and very attractive to investors from areas like California where an 800 sq. ft. property can be priced at a cool million or more. Continue reading and I'm going to explain how property management companies operate when managing properties for investors who live in a different state. Let's start with the difference of an employed property manager and an owner of a property management company. A salaried property manager likely works 9am to 6pm and sometimes Saturdays. Their primary responsibilities are to manage leasing agents, manage tenants, and deal with contractors and other managers. When managing an apartment building the property manager may receive free or extremely low rent. An owner of a property management company primarily works with owners of the properties and top managers. They don't have as much contact with the tenants.

The average salary for a property manager is $30,000 to $50,000 per year. The average property management company has the potential to make $30,000 to $50,000 per month. Now do you see why someone would be a landlord in the owner's absence.

Detroit, Michigan and similar areas such as Cleveland Ohio, and St. Louis, Missouri, are all desirable areas for investors all over the world. Many of these investors buy dozens of houses, which is the cause for significant property management demand. Some of my best clients come from Australia, Argentina, Florida, California, and New York. To start a property management business, a person should have high integrity and a good work ethic; the manager is providing maintenance and collecting rent on the owner's behalf. To own a property management company, you technically need to be licensed by the state with a Broker license, not a real estate agent license but Broker. Many companies are practicing without any license at all because the demand is so high and many investors don't ask for credentials, they just want help. Continue reading and I'll tell you later in this chapter how to get around having a Broker license and work as a property manager anyway. First, let me explain a few important reasons an owner would hire you as a property manager:

1. You have excellent knowledge of the rental property market.

2. You have developed proven policies and procedures for each aspect of property management, such as repairs, tenant selection, and rent collection.

3. You have good contacts and relationships with contractors.

Now, I'd like to explain reasons an owner will keep you as property manager.

» You get and retain the best tenants
» Proper screening of potential renters is a must. The best way to find good tenants is to spread the message through your network. This includes; employer bulletin boards, referrals from other good tenants, referrals from places of worship.
» You care about their property.

Advertising a house online can sometimes be a problem for investors, if the property is vacant. Therefore, owners want a property manager who's experienced and versatile. Let's be honest, the Internet is a gift and a curse. It allows people to find information with the click of a button; the Internet also enables scammers to obtain information and scam faster. This is why a good property manager is knowledgeable enough to know when to post ads about their property online and when to avoid it. Selling or renting offline avoids using the MLS (multiple listing service) which syndicates to more than 300 websites. Sometimes you'll need to find tenants offline through networking and referrals like mentioned before.

Once you've connected with possible good tenants, verify their personal photo identification, check stubs, references, employment history, and get a credit and background check. During my own tenant-landlord days, I had a tenant who was sweet as pie before moving into the house. She had a live-in boyfriend and two children. After they moved in, I learned about her other three children, and she never paid rent. We later learned she was a professional bad tenant. One who never intends to pay rent and moves a few times a year. Needless to say, this was an expensive lesson for me. To top it off, during the eviction, the boyfriend says "I better not catch you anywhere." The nerve of some people! This is when I learned proper tenant screening is a must! This is a step profitable landlords never skip. Furthermore, other reasons an owner will keep you as a property manager include:

» Maintenance – you have contractors and maintenance crews available around the clock to handle emergencies.
» Bids – You're able to generate reasonable repair and rent ready bids in a reasonable amount of time.
» Pricing – You rent the properties at a good market rate. Opposed to letting your friends or family move in at the cheapest possible rate.
» Leasing – You can easily handle residential and commercial lease agreements with adequate terms, length and mediation details.

Thriving property management companies with a lot of units have a good system and a team. They also set expectations of the tenants from day one. Repair and maintenance requests are ordered online and they almost never pick up rent in person.

Profitable property management companies also use very effective messages on advertisements; this usually includes an attractive headline, credit score or income requirements, benefits of the property to the renter, a call to action, and a mention of any move in specials. Lucrative property management companies also know exactly how to handle rent defaulters. Even when you have the best renters, they are not immune to common problems such as unemployment, ill health, divorce, and accidents. If I had to narrow it down, here are the top two ways to deal with tenants who aren't paying and won't leave (with the owner's permission of course):

Discuss a voluntary settlement

Regardless of the tenant's position, it's best to try and settle as courts can be time-consuming, expensive, and frustrating. If you can't come to an agreement with the tenant, be sure to follow the law to legally evict a tenant as you don't want to cause bigger problems for your client. On the other hand, these eviction tactics are not permissible by law;

» Holding on to the renter's personal possessions.
» Turning off the renter's access to basic amenities such as electricity, heat, or water.
» Changing the door's locks.
» Assaulting the tenant.
» Breaking into the property and removing their possessions on your own.

The tenant problems and solutions were brought to your attention because they are done out of frustration. Hence, the reason a licensed broker needs to be involved with a good attorney close by. Many entrepreneurs who want to start a property management company will typically team up with a licensed broker to speed up the process.

In summary, perform these 7 tasks in preparation to start a property management company:

1. Learn the market! Search online to see what rental market prices are per square feet and compare to different neighborhoods and zip codes.

2. Join investment groups to learn more about property management or to network with real estate Brokers.

3. Review rent advertisements online. Analyze the details that grab your attention and compare them to the ads that are easily overlooked.

4. Learn the laws of dealing with rent defaulters.

5. Develop a repeatable process for maintaining the property.

6. Start networking with good contractors.

7. Find a consulting firm to walk you through starting a property management company.

As a person interested in real estate, I am sure you must have heard several heart-touching stories of tenant/landlord relationships GONE WRONG. However, don't let this discourage you from learning to be a property manager. I started a property management company because I work with a lot of overseas investors and sometimes they need help and services that big companies don't offer or have time for. Property management is not a passion for me but is a side hustle. There are 21 ways to make money in real estate but I encourage you to learn as much as you can and discover the one you enjoy.

Empowerment Plan

1. Connect with a real estate broker and ask about job opportunities to show properties to prospective tenants. You can also inquire about job shadowing. Some property managers hire temporary workers to show their properties in exchange for 25% of the first month's rent. This is a great way to learn the business.

2. If you're skilled in manual labor work on properties. Start a property restoration company. You may only get cleaning jobs at first, but it could easily grow into something larger.

3. Start a landscaping company and connect with property managers. Offer to be responsible for keeping the exterior clean and neat during winter or summer months.

WRITE GOALS OR THOUGHTS HERE

_____

_____

_____

_____

_____

_____

_____

_____

_____

_____

_____

_____

_____

_____

_____

_____

_____

_____

_____

_____

_____

_____

_____

_____

CHAPTER 4

FLIPPING LIKE HGTV

Would you like to learn the real truth about flipping houses? This chapter will reveal some of the good and bad secrets that are not shown on HGTV. When thinking of real estate investing, the second most common strategy people learn of is flipping houses. What exactly does flipping houses imply? Buying an ugly property for cheap that needs a bunch of renovations. Then fixing it up to be new, beautiful, and sell for top dollar. Many people believe this to be the most fascinating part of real estate investing. On television, it looks like the glamorous life because they leave out so many details. Continue reading this chapter to learn the good, the bad, and the ugly when flipping houses.

When I think about the good in flipping houses like HGTV, I think of 2012 when I purchased a few houses from the auction. I got lucky enough that two of them only needed fresh paint. I rented the houses and quickly sold them to investors. Both houses were

3-bedroom bricks purchased for less than $10,000 total. Each house was rented for $800 per month. One house sold for $23,000, and the other $25,000. All we did was paint!

When I think of the bad when flipping houses, I think about a time or two when I got in an entanglement with bad contractors. One made an offer I couldn't refuse then ran off with the funds. This same contractor had completed a roof for us in the past, a gutter replacement for one of my clients; but this time he ran off. *Why I thought to myself.* Continue reading and you might understand a bit. Fast forward to months later with bigger and better projects; some contractors said they could do the job, showed pictures and videos of prior work, but in the end, they just weren't skilled. What I later learned is that contractors might show work of other contractors who were on the job with them. I've had many good and bad experiences with contractors which is why I study their tactics so closely. My biggest lesson learned about hiring contractors is to get referrals from good contractors who might be too busy for your project. I learned that most good contractors know each other. But hardly anyone knows the bad contractors. I speak freely about my unfortunate contractor situations today because they made me sharp. There was a time I was too embarrassed to share these stories but sharing is caring. I'd like to help someone avoid a bad contractor so they aren't experimenting on your dime.

Last but not least, when I think of the ugly part of flipping houses, one of my biggest failures comes to mind. Let's just call it *"The Monica Project."* When I tell you everything went wrong, ***everything went wrong***! This failure even caused me to sign up for school to get my builders license. I had it all planned out. First I wanted the new roof put on. Second, I wanted kitchen and bath gutted and remodeled. Last wanted fresh paint throughout and hardwood floors finished. My first mistake was not recognizing the budget would not allow us to reach our end goal which was to sell top dollar. The project plan should have been altered when investor and I didn't agree on renovation budget; but hindsight is 20/20. I'll spare you every little detail about what went wrong but I will explain our major turning points. The first head contractor was referred to me by a friend and I visited a house to see his work. He seemed very easy to work with and somewhat professional until after the first payment. Him and his guys started missing days, not answering telephone calls, and eventually needed to be replaced after too many "no shows" and a bunch of excuses. One excuse was his phone fell off the roof. The second tile guy talked a good game but overall had poor craftsmanship and lacked experience. Before I hired the second contractor, he showed me lots of videos in his phone of big projects he had worked on in the area. I later learned the videos and pictures were not his work. They couldn't have been after seeing the results he gave me. Long story short, *"The Monica Project"* turned out to be a bust! I was the most disappointed I had been my whole real estate career. I fought for that project until the end. I even sent my assistant there to watch them if I wasn't present. Again, the experience helped shape me into the project manager I am today. A few weeks after the big disappointment on *The Monica Project*, I took 2.5 weeks off from selling real estate to go to school and learn how to become a licensed builder. I was hungry to learn why I had so many problems working with contractors and getting houses renovated on time. Continue reading and you will understand what I learned in builder school.

How to increase success and reduce problems when renovating a house for flipping:

1. Have the right budget or change the plan. Cheaper isn't always better when renovating a house. Some of the most expensive contractors in our area do the best work and their quality shows. Hiring a cheaper contractor may force you to do the work twice.

2. Be prepared to show up at the property while the contractors work or have an experienced project manager available to check in. Let's be honest. Many contractors have to work with lots of people to earn a living. If nobody is ever at your house, they might be working at a different property where someone is watching.

3. Hire a specialist! When contractors tell you they do everything, be sure to ask what they specialize in or what they do the best. If he says he's great at

interior and exterior painting, that should be his only responsibility. Not laying bathroom tile.

Speaking of hiring a specialist; remember the contractor I spoke of earlier who gave a price I couldn't refuse then ran off with the funds? The contractor had done exterior work for me and a client in the past. When he ran off, the job was for interior work and he subcontracted the work out to people who were clearly not dependable. Maybe this is why he ran off. Whatever the reason, it's shameful!

There are so many things that can go wrong when flipping houses like HGTV. Hopefully learning my dreadful experiences will help someone. *Sometimes you win, sometimes you learn* is my motto.

Renovations and working with contractors can be lucrative or can be a nightmare depending on the project managers level of experience. I always say *"every house has a secret,"* so when the plan changes, your plan needs to change too. When rehabbing starts, the house secrets usually get exposed and that's when the adjustments should start. Modifications can hinder your renovation plans and budgeting completely. How big or small the secret is, will determine what you should eliminate, adjust, or if you need more funding. Many times, more funding is not an option.

Levels to Flipping

Just like REALTORS, there are so many different heights that house flippers can aim for. Some only rehab properties with an ARV under $250,000. The reason for this is because $150,000 to $250,000 is a very common price that growing families purchase at in Metro Detroit. These houses and price ranges tend to sell quickly. A different level of house flippers may only renovate luxury properties at $450,000 and above or build new construction. Next you have flippers who like properties between $60,000 and $150,000 because they sell super-fast in metro Detroit. Next you have flippers who follow a strategy of buying properties with no more than 1,600 sq ft. It's big enough for a family of 4 but small enough to keep cost down during renovations. You see larger houses take longer to renovate. Therefore, holding costs are higher (heat and electricity); ultimately driving down your potential profit. Oh and by the way, those $1,000 homes you see online are not what they seem. I've noticed many newer investors don't calculate the rehab amount or think about the time they'll spend with repairs. Once they do, it no longer looks like a good deal. REALTORS are Empowered through Real Estate when working with house flippers because they can learn how to properly estimate rehab cost and after repair value. Project managers are empowered when on a rehab job because they play the role of a general contractor. This job can be a handful and you'll need, to play politics with contractors, and have the courage to fire them when necessary. After dabbling in various types of real estate businesses, I've had many conversations with myself. What I've realized is that I like selling houses, and flipping contracts over renovating houses because of all the time and contractors involved in flipping. *We will go into detail about flipping contracts in the next chapter.*

Back to the builders course I took after *The Monica Project.* It felt refreshing and empowering to get professional advice on the do's and don'ts when renovating. It also felt good to learn that women aren't the only ones having problems with contractors while renovating houses. I started studying for the exam immediately after the course. The first half (the business side) was a breeze. The second half of studying for the exam felt like torture. They actually wanted me to know how to build a house; from pouring the foundation to installing walls, and roof soffits. I decided that my time would be best used growing in the areas of real estate that I already enjoy and do well. Again, there are 21 ways to make money in real estate. I believe people should do what comes natural for them and what they enjoy. Before I introduce you to someone who is an expert in flipping houses like HGTV, I'd like to give a few more red flags about working with contractors:

1. Beware of contractors under 50 years old who don't have Facebook or Instagram pages. They may be hiding from people they have ripped off.

2. If you plan to be a full-time project manager for fix and flips, beware of getting referrals from regular people. Try to get recommendations from good contractors who might be too busy to start your project. The good ones usually hang in the same circle. Additionally, everyday people may not understand the difference between a handy man, a mediocre contractor, and a contractor who does quality work for a flip.

3. Hire contractors who specialize in specific jobs for best quality. For instance, if a contractor has a company called Charlie's Painting, let him paint and that's it. They will likely hire sub-contractors to do floors or windows. You can subcontract the work yourself.

4. If there is no meeting of the minds about budgeting when working as a project manager, it's best to decline the job. Budgeting and knowing your numbers is a big enough challenge. Set yourself up for success from the beginning!

Furthermore, understanding how to find and buy a property below market value, and determine the right ARV (after repair value) takes a lot of skill. This makes me think about Rochelle Nelson of SYMRHO Investments. She knows her numbers, has the vision, and understands how to work well with contractors.

Rochelle does rehabs right!

Rochelle is a retired school teacher, now a millionaire real estate investor. Teaching was her first passion. When she was a little girl, she would teach kids in the neighborhood whatever she could. Rochelle learned real estate from her father.

He was a licensed contractor and real estate investor who owned many properties. She would always be with him as he collected rent. Her father also owned Mitchell's house of bars. His company-built bars at the popular Detroit night clubs Floods Bar and Grill, and Bakers Lounge. Her father was very adamant about Rochelle getting a college degree; he didn't really want her in the real estate field since it can be so cut throat. This could be the reason Rochelle couldn't stop thinking about the possibilities in real estate. One day at the age of 21, Rochelle decided to buy a house at an auction. She took $30,000 that she had saved and purchased her first house on Strathmoor st. in Detroit. She bought it sight unseen, paid a bunch of crazy fees but was determined to flip it. While gathering materials at Home Depot, she met a guy and had a conversation about renovating the property. The guy completed the whole house for her. She put $8,000 into the house and paid the

Home Depot guy $7,000. Rochelle later sold the house for $125,000 and made a $80,000 profit.

Rochelle took that $80,000, moved on, and purchased another house on Cherrylawn St. She bought it for $45,000, renovated it, flipped it, and doubled the money. She just kept going and going, buying, flipping, buying, and flipping. That $30,000 easily turned into a million dollars within 5 years.

Advice from Rochelle: Evaluate, reflect, then DO. Reflect and review your passions. That will help you understand what you're good at. To find your passion, think about what you would do for free. Money will come if you're passionate about something.

Rochelle says "starting a business right now is so much easier because of social media. There are a lot of resources and ways to find workers in Facebook groups to get tasks completed quickly." "If you're scared, a great way to get started is to network and partner up with people."

What does being empowered through real estate mean to Rochelle? It means opportunities to build passive income; she says real estate is the fastest way to build wealth. Buying property, holding, renting it out will even give passive income during a recession if you get section 8 tenants.

"When I was growing up and saw my father buy real estate and go house to house collecting rent, it taught me something. The main way I'm empowered through real estate is because it helps me collect revenue and build a real estate legacy for my daughter."

Rochelle believes her real estate business is more successful than others because she's very selective about tenants. Most of her tenants use section 8 vouchers. She has real conversations with them and wants to know where they plan to go in life. She wants to understand their mindset and if they are trying to use section 8 as a stepping stone to improve their lives and do better in life eventually becoming an owner.

Rochelle's biggest lesson learned: being young and paying all cash for a brand-new Lexus LS430. I could hardly use the car, especially during the winter because I was always working on houses. I paid all that money for a car but was consistently renting trucks to move housing materials. I paid $56,000 for that car and sold it for $10,000. "I kept thinking DAMN! That money could have been used to buy a house." The car depreciated while her houses were appreciating. Continue reading and look at some Before and After pictures of Rochelle's projects.

What advice would you give someone afraid to step out on faith?

I was very young when I retired as a school teacher and I remember telling other teachers to buy real estate. Find someone who is a little less afraid than you are. Find a few people who are a little braver about the investing process and you'll have less worry and less of a loss should something go wrong. A team is also helpful for resources and encouraging each other; this helps build confidence too. Eventually, your anxiety and fear will ease up and you'll start helping others or investing on your own.

Final Words of wisdom from Rochelle: You can't lose in real estate. Even when you take a financial loss, you should gain knowledge of how to do it better next time.

After

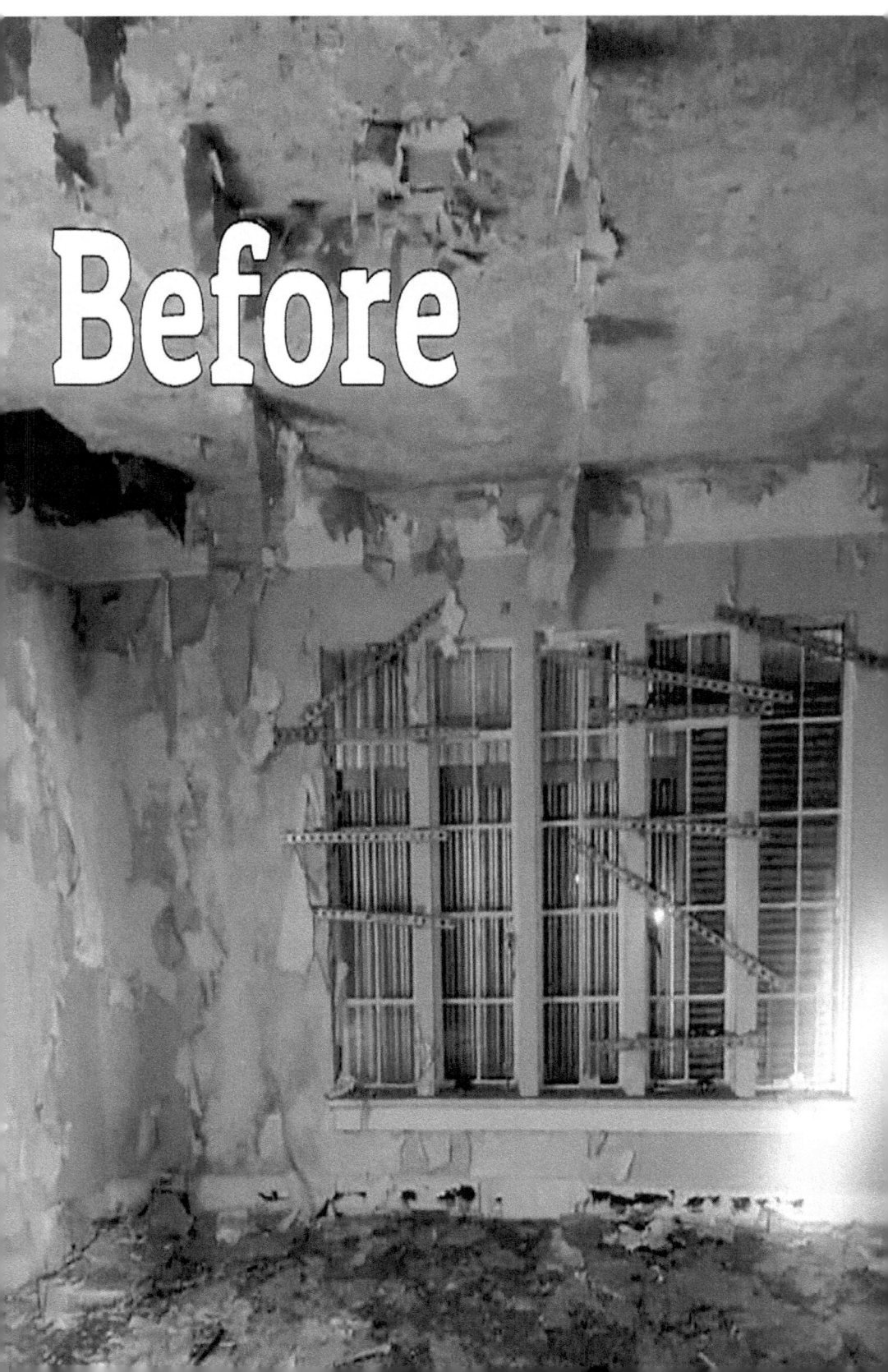
Before

After

Before

After!

Before

After

SYMRHO INVESTMENTS

Rochelle Nelson
401- 830 3328

By now you might be wondering, how can I find good deals to flip like HGTV?

- » MLS (multiple listing service) from REALTOR
- » Real estate investment groups online and in person
- » Probate sales
- » Tax auctions
- » Online auctions
- » Probate and divorce attorneys
- » A professional prospector (cold caller)

Now, you've learned more about the good, the bad, and the ugly when Flipping Houses like HGTV. Continue reading this book and we'll look at some real estate investing strategies you can do *without* dealing with contractors or tenants.

CHAPTER 5

IF YOU CAN'T BEAT THEM, JOIN THEM

Picture this! February 2020 before we were aware Covid-19 was in the United States. Hundreds of distinguished black people met in midtown Atlanta Georgia, at Loews hotel for a real estate investing conference. After a rocky morning plane ride through a rain storm, I was relieved to make it to the hotel safely. I put my luggage in the room, freshened up, and started roaming the halls to see the activities and setup for the conference. I was really excited and had no idea what to expect. As I roamed through the halls, I was surprised at how quiet it was. There were not a lot of people around and I thought to myself "this conference is going to suck, where is everyone?" Finally, I started to see a person or two walking the halls and I would ask questions and they would point. As I walked to the door to peek inside, I saw the largest conference room table ever in a room of about 50 people. It was very private and exclusive!

At fi rst glance, I made eye contact with the man himself Max Maxwell of Wholesaling Elite and I quickly shut the door out of embarrassment. I realized this day was for mastermind tickets holders only. Up close and personal training from the speakers! Right then and there I recognized what a huge mistake I made *being cheap*. The disappointment of not purchasing a mastermind ticket lead me to; roam the halls a little more, walk midtown Atlanta sight-seeing, and search for good restaurants with carbs and cocktails so I could pout. I was eager, but patiently waited for the conference to start for general ticket holders.

Wholesaling houses is what I call "flipping contracts." It is an old investment exit strategy that has become extremely popular within the last few years. I say extremely popular because everyone you know is doing it from grandfathers to 18 year olds. Have you ever heard of "real estate investing with no money?" This is another term you might hear when someone speaks of wholesaling houses. To explain it in detail, when someone wants to sell a house As-Is for cash, a wholesaler submits their offer, gets the seller to sign the agreement, then finds a buyer. I started practicing this technique after giving away one too many flip deals as a REALTOR and the generosity wasn't returned.

Let's get back to the real estate conference in Atlanta. The next morning I saw hundreds of distinguished looking black and brown people arriving. Today was the big day! The hallways were filled with approximately 80% men and 20% women. About 85% of the people were African American, I saw a handful of

Hispanic people and a few Caucasians; all hungry to learn more about real estate investing; it was a BEAUTIFUL sight! On the first day, speakers literally stayed in the conference room coaching us until 9 pm, 3 hours later than conference should have ended. I've attended dozens of real estate conferences in the past 7 years, and I've never seen this happen. I smiled and thought to myself "I'm glad I took a chance on something different; this conference is one of a kind and will be life changing for me."

Day 2, I experienced the same vibe; approximately 500 to 600 beautiful people, networking, learning, and happy to be there. On this day, one of the speakers said a few things I'll never forget. He said, and I quote, "wholesaling is done in every industry (i.e., automotive, liquor, t-shirts, everything). But why is it frowned upon when wholesaling is done in real estate?" I thought to myself, he's right! I remembered how it took some time for me to adjust my mindset about the wholesaling concept. Many licensed real estate agents believe that wholesaling is unethical or illegal because real estate school teaches to help the homeowner sell their property for the most money possible. I've learned that *sometimes convenience is more important than top dollar for homeowners*. Additionally, many REALTORS have to understand the difference of top dollar for a house that's completely updated, compared to top dollar for a house that hasn't been updated in 20 years. These are skills learned by working with investors and going through a lot of houses. With Zillow recently announcing they are going to become a licensed brokerage, many REALTORS are concerned about losing their value. Many other REALTORS are fighting back by getting more creative and learning new skills like wholesaling houses.

Adjusting to wholesaling will likely be easier for agents who have been working with investors already. Additionally, he or she must be extremely careful and have all their I's dotted and T's crossed when wholesaling a house. Learning wholesaling is a good skill to have for people working in urban areas. The city is where the most people are often faced with challenges that require them to get cash fast. In many situations, they don't want to wait on a REALTOR to put their house on the market. Also, some homeowners in urban areas don't believe people with credentials such as a REALTOR license can get a house sold quickly for cash. Sounds funny doesn't it? This was told to me directly from a homeowner. I believe this type of thinking comes from what we see on television. Or after speaking to many different REALTORS who don't usually visit vacant houses that need repair. See there are so many different types of REALTORS, over 12,000 in metro Detroit, and most people don't know how to seek out the **Investor REALTOR**. Furthermore, a REALTOR who works with retail buyers (families who will live in the property) and retail sellers (families who will fix their house up to sell for top dollar), may not know how to get a house sold fast for cash. These are just a few reasons it's tough to understand REALTORS.

How much would you pay for security and convenience?

At first, it was difficult for me to understand why a homeowner might choose a wholesaler over REALTOR. The first reason is, homeowners don't know that the person is a wholesaler. The second reason is security and convenience. Let me take you back to 2014 before I started wholesaling. Picture this! *I'm at a listing appointment talking to a sweet old lady. She was ready to move forward with me, and I remember asking her, "how can we handle showings when someone wants to view the house?" She paused and decided she wanted to think about it a little more and get back to me. I followed up with her a day or two later, and she said, "I signed with an investor directly because I don't want to deal with all the showings." I'll never forget she sold the house for $10,000 less than what I was going to sell the house for. That's when I learned that sometimes, people will pay big money for convenience and to feel more secure.*

Disappointment after disappointment, I continued to receive similar responses from homeowners about not wanting different people in their house. I realized the idea of expanding my business needed to happen immediately. I thought to myself, the wholesaler is literally doing the same tasks that a listing agent REALTOR would do. The key difference is the privacy and exclusivity offered. I made changes to my business model and started an LLC. That way I was not using my real estate license when performing the wholesaling investment strategy. To sum it up, wholesaling is finding a property that has equity. And getting the owner to agree at a selling at a price below market value. For instance, you and the owner come to a price of $25,000 for a house. Then you find a new buyer who will pay $35,000. The strategy is simple but not easy. As of today, Michigan does not require a license to wholesale houses.

However, in 2019, Illinois passed a law requiring a real estate license for wholesaling houses. This law might be coming to Michigan soon. Since my primary clientele are home sellers and I perform duties of a Listing Agent, wholesaling wasn't that difficult for me to come to terms with. The listing agent REALTOR and Wholesaler have similar duties. They both visit houses or analyze the value of the house by reviewing online data. They both perform a lot of online advertising duties, and they both get a contract signed. The primary difference is that the REALTOR puts the property on the MLS to find a buyer. The wholesaler finds a buyer privately through email and networking. I personally don't advise anyone to put a property under contract if they don't already know the buyer or have the funds to really buy the property for cash. Furthermore, REALTORS need to be extremely careful when submitting cash offers to homeowners as their license could be at risk if not done correctly.

Let me take you back again to the real estate conference in Atlanta. I was surprised to learn all the time and effort that goes into generating leads with bandit signs. You know those signs that you see on the corners "we buy houses?" These signs are designed to generate leads and the signs work well for many investors. I found it interesting to learn that these signs aren't stapled to the pole just one time; they are stapled a few times a week. These signs are often removed by city workers and some cities will fine the person. Some wholesalers also use different phone numbers to know which location the lead was generated from when someone calls. I've tried bandit signs many times in the past with little success. Therefore, I don't bother today. At the conference in Atlanta, many successful wholesalers also discussed partnering up and working in teams; similar to how big real estate agent teams do. If an investor/wholesaler is not a licensed real estate agent, they usually will have someone licensed on their team to increase victory. In summary, some of my biggest takeaways from the conference regarding systems were to:

1. Master the motivated seller script, objection handlers, and never skip the pre-qualifying questions.

2. Team up with bird dogs to help drive for dollars more often.

3. Choose two or three lead generation tools that have worked and stick to them.

Let's go into more detail about pre-qualifying questions. This is key to avoid wasting time, gas, and effort. The last thing you'll have time for is to view a house and talk to owners who aren't really motivated to sell. I've learned the hard way which is why I always ask the following questions (*in a conversational tone*) before going to an appointment.

- » When do you need to be moved by?
- » May I ask where you are moving to? (If they say, "I don't know yet, this could be a red flag). They could be hiding something.
- » Do you need assistance finding a new place?
- » When I arrive to view the house, will all decision makers be present?
- » Do you owe any backed taxes or mortgages on the property?

Simple questions like this will help you quickly understand if a homeowner is really motivated to sell, or testing the waters to try getting an unreasonable price. Pre-screening buyers is also an essential skill to learn when working as a REALTOR, or investor. Understanding the types of buyer you have and categorizing them will prevent a lot of wasted time. Continue reading and learn how I use an excel spreadsheet with tabs to categorize buyers.

- » Landlord - Buy and hold cash buyer.
- » Rehabber buyer – people who will fix up the property and flip it quickly.
- » Retail buyer – Financing to live in and love the home.

» Best buyers (this list will be short) - These are your buyers who act quickly, and they have a full database of cash buyers.

» Wholesaling buyer - People who will put the property under contract, and quickly sell it to a buyer. Or do a small amount of work, and put it on the market with a REALTOR.

You might be wondering, why would an investor buy a property, do a little work, then put the property on the MLS? This strategy is called wholetailing. The difference between a wholesale deal and a wholetail deal is wholesale is usually sold off market. Wholetail is sold on market to another investor. I've done this strategy long before I knew it had a name. Wholetail deals are still sold at a deep discount and the investor typically does minor work like a junk removal clean out, then they sell it to a flipper. You'll be amazed to learn how sometimes a house just needs a good clean out or clean up to sell for $15,000 more than it sold for a week prior.

This makes me think of Deonte and Devona Johnson. They are the owners of 'All I do is Junk' and 'Quality Cleaning Connection'. Their companies work magic for wholesalers and short term investors.

They are a spiritual family and are the definition of stepping out on faith. Deonte and Devona met in high school but never connected until many years after graduation. Their business idea was born as a result of a bad car accident. Devona had worked in Corporate America her whole adult life. She had a car accident one day on her way home from work, which resulted in back surgery. During that time, Devona was on FMLA, and was eventually terminated by her employer.

As Devona started to recover, one of her friends had a property management business and needed help. Devona decided to work for one week to help out. One day as unexpected problems kept happening, contractors didn't get a property cleaned out for a very important client and showing. Devona, her husband, and two sons decided to go above and beyond her job duties and clean the property out themselves. The property was disgusting and filled with trash from years of being abandoned.

After a lot of hard work and seeing the beauty of this property after the clean out, Deonte told his wife; maybe we should start a business like this. Devona thought the idea was crazy. Deonte and Davona always talked about starting a business but never imagined junk removal and cleaning.

Eventually she was convinced to try and the rest is history.

Devona would message everyone she knew through

Facebook and texting to tell them about their new business. She joined investment groups on Facebook and every chance she could, she'd promote her company without being too pushy. She just wanted everyone to know what her company offered. Eventually, these people started to refer them and tag them when someone asked for a property clean out company. Within 12 months, Deonte and Devona were known as the best company to call for Detroit property clean outs. They were told by many real estate professionals "they had the clean out business ON LOCK". Meaning everyone wanted to hire their company to clean out residential and commercial properties. They had created a stellar reputation fast and were growing even faster!

Deonte says their secret sauce is that "Customer service is not dead!" They strive hard to meet the customer's needs. And they like to follow up to make sure people are satisfied.

Deonte is a natural giver, and he always wants to make sure the client is happy and satisfied when he does a job. Deonte's background was retail management and truck driving. Treating customers with respect and letting them feel good about spending money is his goal.

What does being empowered through real estate means to Deonte and Devona?

» Building wealth and something tangible to pass on to their children.
» Making life long personal and business relationships.
» Unlimited possibilities

Words of wisdom from Devona: *I never imagined our business would take off as fast as it did. Don't doubt yourself! You have no idea what's in you.*

Deonte's words of wisdom: *Trust the process, trust the stage that you're in, and keep improving.*

To contact the Johnsons for junk removal or
quality cleaning, visit AlliDoisJunk.com

Now that you've learned what happens to properties that are purchased at a discount, continue reading to learn more creative ways to invest in real estate.

Empowerment Plan:

1. Find property managers and see what openings they have. This is a great way to learn different aspects of real estate investing.

2. Create a good script for motivated sellers.

3. Start cold calling or texting for business and listen attentively.

4. Call or mail postcards to addresses of recently deceased people to find motivated sellers.

5. Run advertisements targeting tired landlords.

6. Join real estate investment groups on Facebook.

WRITE GOALS OR THOUGHTS HERE

CHAPTER 6

FROM KFC TO AFC

I n the last chapter you learned about Deonte and Devona's journey on quickly growing their junk removal company. The primary business purpose was to clean out old houses that had been abandoned for years. Their second company Quality Cleaning Connection is currently growing even faster because of the short term rental business (aka Airbnb). In 2018 I noticed a lot of buzz about short term rentals in Michigan. Honestly, I thought to myself "who would need a short term rental in Detroit, why not just get a hotel?" Boy have times changed and I've learned a lot. Consumers of today choose short rentals over hotels because they off er more space, peace, and sometimes a unique experience. I also learned that people travel to Detroit for all sorts of reasons, not just real estate investing. Although people are starting to travel again (post Covid), (well they are as I'm editing this book); I still think I dodged bullet! I had been researching and studying the short term rental business for a few years. Toward the end of 2019, I was just about ready to pull the trigger and launch. I found a nice, quiet location in Detroit bordering a suburb. It was small enough to keep cost low, but big enough to be much better than a hotel. With changes in the hospitality field as a result of Covid-19 this is one venture I'm glad I didn't execute quickly on. I'm sure the industry will recover but will it have the same demand as it had pre Covid-19?

Let's look at the numbers and why short-term rentals got my attention in the first place. The average cost to rent a 3 bedroom house in Detroit is $800 per month. The average earnings in 2019 for short term rental businesses were $2,500 to $4,000 per month. After a few years of research, I interviewed several people in real estate who were kind enough to give me inside information and take my calls with questions. The short-term rental business can be stable and lucrative if done the right way. Consumers utilize short term rentals for many different reasons, not just tourism. Below are the top 5:

1. Waiting on a new construction home to get completed
2. Music video shoot
3. Repast ceremony after a funeral
4. Cheat on their mate
5. Explore a new neighborhood before buying

During my research journey learning about short term rentals, I watched countless videos, listened to 3 audio books, joined a few top Facebook groups, and planned to take over. After all that studying and learning, I slowed down to make sure it would be a good side hustle for me. My real estate business keeps me extremely busy; sometimes I have to be available for people at any time of day from 9am through 9pm. Although I didn't personally experience the short-term rental business, 1 learned plenty from the conversations in groups. One issue that turned me away was "instant bookings" linked to credit card scams. Another common complaint I learned about was patrons taking the whole drawer of coffee K-cups that were meant for each guest for the next 30 days. Then there were the owners upset that patrons consistently damaged sheets, needed earlier or later check outs, and more. Late check outs can cause big problems as it delays for house cleaners to do their job in a timely manner to prepare for the next guest. Just the other day, there was a post in one of the short-term rental groups where a business owner was very upset about the lack of response from one of the technology companies. Three years ago, her place was trashed, the renter had a big party in her property, and the company she used to book them did not pay her for the damages. She needed advice about how to handle it. Can you believe the majority of responses stated to put the company on blast via social media; to go on Twitter and tag the company? These are the types of horror stories that made me take a step back to really decide if it was something I wanted to do or had time for. It no longer looked like a side hustle, but a full-time job with many problems. I tell you these horror stories because they will help you to make a decision on the type of investing that might be best for you. I know that cameras and other security measures can help you avoid some of these problems, but it's still powerful to know the good, bad, and ugly of a business. I always tell people, *there are 21 ways to make money in real estate, but that doesn't mean you should do them all.*

Let's take a look at three other real estate related businesses where owners work closely with the patron.

1. *A halfway house* is an institution for recently incarcerated people to live and be monitored as they slowly transition back into the real world. Some houses provide instructional living skills for independent living. The income generated for halfway houses varies depending on the tenants selected to live inside and if they are paying cash or receiving government assistance.

2. *A Veteran Home* is a facility that basically provides care for veterans. State veteran homes have application processes that could take a couple of weeks or even months. Veterans with special disabilities may receive financial compensation; however most veterans with income pay their share of the cost. But for veterans who have service-connected disabilities, may get a contribution from the government, which in most areas is more than enough to settle their home cost, reducing out of pocket cost for them.

3. **Adult foster care homes** (AFC) are where older adults who no longer have the ability to live independently reside. The home usually offers special services needed in exchange for payment. Assistance and support provided at adult foster care homes might include:

» Preparation of meal and assistance with eating
» Laundry
» Bathing
» Dressing
» Walking
» Managing medication
» Running errands

The businesses mentioned thus far are what real estate professionals might consider income properties. When a property is purchased with the goal of generating monthly revenue, they are referred to as income or investment properties. One type of income property that does _not_ consist of caring for anyone else are multi-family units. A popular strategy today for new investors is to purchase a multi-family property, then live in one unit and rent the other. This is an easier way to start generating passive income.

Let's go back to the adult foster care business. This makes me think of Tracey Spencer.

Tracey is the perfect example of believing in self and making things happen. Her real estate journey started right around when the big mortgage crisis was happening in 2007.

Tracey was a full time registered nurse who liked to buy and flip houses for fun. She had just one more house to flip when she started noticing the real estate market changing. She couldn't seem to sell this last house. Every time she got a buyer, something would go wrong toward the end and the mortgage lender would say the buyer no longer qualified. Banks were declining buyers left and right last minute. After a lot of time had passed, and money was wasted on inspections Tracey started to feel discouraged and needed a different strategy. After becoming exhausted of all the buyers financing falling through, her mom came up with the idea to start an AFC home.

This was a completely new experience for Tracey so she hired a consultant. Unfortunately, Tracey was ripped off and taken advantage of which made her think maybe the AFC home wasn't the right idea. With no solid buyers for the house and the real estate market getting worse, she noticed prices declining all the way to $5,000 and $6,000. These were not your average 900 sq ft bungalows selling for these low prices; these were houses near historic Boston Edison district in Detroit. Tracey couldn't stand the thought of selling her house at such a low price; she decided the AFC home HAD TO BE A SUCCESS. She even started to buy more houses!

First, she applied to get a state license for the house. Then she learned when you first get certified you have only 6 months to get a client or you'll get shut down. Tracey did not realize how challenging it would be to get client contracts. Tracey was in her early 20's when making all these ambitions moves. She saw a lot of corruption, under the table bribes, and people being taken advantage of; all because they wanted to help people. Soon Tracey began to really understand that old saying, it's not always what you know but who you know. Tracey continued to fear being shut down. During the waiting period, she sought out additional training to work with the mentally ill. This is where things took a turn for her. This training course is where Tracey met Mr. Evans. He had operated his own company and worked in the adult foster care business for quite some time. He took a liking to Tracey and was kind enough to give her the inside scoop. She learned that this was bigger than her trade and nobody cared about her degree or certificate in helping mentally ill patients. While staying faithful and hopeful, Tracey continued to work hard and learn as much as she could about the adult foster care business. One day out of the blue she got a call from Mr. Evans. He had contacted a head person in charge at a company that could give her client contracts. A meeting was scheduled and when Tracey walked in the door, the contract was already in place. Tracey's networking skills, kindness, and determination, landed her the first client. The rest is history!!! This is a prime example of why they say "you never know who will help you so be kind to everyone."

Tracey's background: Before nursing school, she was a shift manager at Kentucky Fried Chicken - That's right, KFC. She was making approx $20,000 a year and was proud of her blue shirt. After a while she became a full time nursing student and it was becoming a very intense program. She asked if she could please work weekends and offered to work doubles so she could concentrate on school during the weekdays. She had haters on the job who complained that her working weekends only was not fair. The head manager at KFC gave Tracey an ultimatum. He told her she would have to work throughout the week and weekends like everyone else, or give up her blue shirt. Tracey was hired in as a manager and could not imagine herself working as a regular fast food employee. She thought about it over and over because she enjoyed her job. Finally her boyfriend helped her make a decision to give up the job and focus on school. She did just that!

After graduating nursing school the first thing Tracey did to celebrate all her hard work was purchase a convertible, red Camaro. She remembers going straight to KFC, driving up to the drive thru window and being shocked that her haters still worked there. She even asked them "WOW! ya'll still work here - Oh okay, I would like a 6 piece hot wing please."

Tracey was pleased with her nursing job and even made $90,000 her first year. She was helping save lives and not even able to drink yet, being under the age of 21. Tracey worked as a registered nurse for approximately 6 years and contingent after her adult foster care home businesses grew.

To this day, Tracey's companies have serviced over 1,000 patients and many are like family to her. Tracey's first AFC home started in 2008 and Home Health Care Company shortly after. The AFC home allowed her to save $120,000 cash to show Medicare and launch the Health Care Company. Tracey has 6 patients per house at the AFC homes and Home Health Care generates $2,000,000 annually. She employs over 30 workers including RN's,

LPN's CNA's, Physical Therapists, Social Workers, and Office Staff.

After years of making a difference in people's lives, Tracey knows all the agony was worth it. She told herself "I MUST succeed" and she did. Tracey is a visionary because she saw the real estate market declining and still made a decision to buy more homes for adult foster care patients she didn't have yet. She laid a foundation and prepared herself to receive what she wanted.

What would Tracey tell someone thinking about starting an AFC home?

1. Don't be afraid to INVEST IN YOURSELF, just believe.

2. Talk your blessings into existence.

3. The income is steady and consistent if you start with a group home.

4. Start networking with other nurses, physical therapists, home care aids, social workers and speech therapists if you're thinking about a home care business.

5. You don't need to be an RN for a home care business, but the background will give an advantage.

Tracey's favorite quote: *Sometimes you have to give it all up to gain something new.*

What does being empowered through real estate mean to Tracey?

Generational wealth! Tracey says there are so many avenues you can do through real estate. You can employ family and improve their lives. She tells her nieces and nephews to act like her business is their business because one day it will be.

What's Tracey's newest venture? She launched a swim wear company. Learn more about these products or shop at SabarrieSwimWear.com.

CHAPTER 7

WHO'S ON YOUR TEAM?

The people you surround yourself with matt er so much when building a real estate business. There are many highs and lows that occur before you see SOLD posts on social media. Having a remarkable team helps keep the motivation and enthusiasm going. Being empowered isn't just about knowing it all or always winning. It's about getting up each time you get knocked down and learning from mistakes. People become empowered when they overcome failures; becoming better and greater after a mistake or two, or three. Let me tell you about a few times I had no choice except to take a loss. Several different times, while trying to build a team and grow, I'm guilty of selecting improper people to invest in. Most of my failures have happened when hiring assistants in my real estate business, or the wrong contractors when trying to fi x and flip a house. Several times I've been asked why I don't seek out friends and family when hiring. I tried that, got lucky once, not so lucky when I hired my son. It lasted about a week and I had to let him go be great at what he's good at doing; opposed to me trying to force him to work the family business. Furthermore, I'd rather keep my good relationships with family and friends. I've learned through trial and error that it is best to seek the right skill set, don't seek a friend! Choosing the wrong people can set you back financially, and/or damage your relationships, or reputation.

The REALTOR'S Hustle

As a real estate sales agent for the last 8 years, I've realized that many spectators love to count a REALTOR'S commission. Some believe REALTORS are overpaid and don't do much to earn the commission. Others perceive REALTORS as money machines who are too cocky or boastful. One thing I can assure you is that REALTORS perform a lot of duties, take abuse, and spend a lot of time and/or money to get properties sold. These are things REALTORS never talk about it; they just DO IT! Let's discuss what it takes to get and sell one house. Many REALTORS call or text people for three hours each day to find new business. REALTORS that specialize in listing properties will call neighborhoods, people they know from church or family, they also call people they don't know who might be thinking about selling. People they don't know are expired listings, neighborhoods, other businesses, or for sale by owners (FSBO's). To obtain these lists, REALTORS pay for systems on a monthly basis and phone dialers to call more people faster. Additionally, other ways they find a house to sell are online advertising, postcard mailers, and networking.

There are many ways to find a house, just know it's not always easy.

Step 1: Once a REALTOR finds a potential house to sell, they check comps on the multiple listing service (MLS). This will give an idea what the house is worth based on similar sold properties.

Step 2: the REALTOR usually goes on an appointment to meet the owner and see the house and explain the marketing strategy. This can be dangerous so the REALTOR must perform a lot of due diligence in advance to make sure they are speaking to the actual owner of the property. An alternative to visiting the house is a virtual meeting using video call and having the client walk through the house.

Step 3: REALTOR agrees to a selling price with the seller and gets the listing agreement signed.

Step 4: REALTOR hires and schedules a photographer to take pictures of the house.

Step 5: house gets a sign out and lockbox if it is vacant or arranges inside access with owner.

Step 6: house is entered into the MLS and marketing/promotions are arranged.

Step 7: house goes LIVE for the world to see.

Step 8: REALTOR takes many phone calls and emails from potential buyers and agents answering questions about the house.

Step 9: once an offer is received on the house, REALTOR analyzes the offer and helps seller negotiate if necessary.

Step 10: title search is ordered through third party.

Step 11: inspection is scheduled for the buyer.

Step 12: possible additional negotiations if buyer saw problems from inspection.

Step 13: appraisal scheduled if buyer is purchasing with financing.

Step 14: final walk through and prepare for closing. Although I mentioned a lot of steps, there are still many challenges that could happen between each step.

Sometimes these 14 steps happen two or three times before the REALTOR sees one penny of a payment. Sounds crazy, doesn't it? So now you might understand that when you see that sold sign, the REALTOR has earned the right to share that proud moment with the world.

I bet by now your thinking why would anyone want to do this and how could they keep going? I always compare a REALTOR to a quarterback in football. The REALTOR creates a plan and gets the glory. But they couldn't do it without a great team. It's time to put a spotlight on the important people and small businesses who work closely with REALTORS to make transactions happen. No real estate license is required to perform these duties. The first role essential to a REALTOR is the personal assistant. This person helps to coordinate showings, makes and takes phone calls on the REALTOR'S behalf, drives to houses to put on and pick up lockboxes, creates listing presentations, and so much more. Real estate assistants show up wearing many different hats; sometimes performing 3 or 4 different job tasks at a time. **The virtual assistant** typically performs administrative duties from home or a different location that is not inside the real estate office. Typically, they type contacts into a database, organize the CRM (customer relationship manager) software, and perform skip tracing, MLS research, make phone calls, and send emails. The tasks for a virtual assistant are somewhat limited compared to what a personal assistant in the office does. When a REALTOR hires a **personal assistant,** they can't just choose any person. The assistant works very closely with the REALTOR and need a diverse range of skills. An essential task performed by assistants is preparation of presentations for listing appointments. When a homeowner wants to sell a property, research and data are usually carried out and collected respectively in advance. A CMA (comparative market analysis) is developed to determine the best price to market the home. Secondly, a listing presentation is prepared in an attempt for agents and homeowners to stay on track making it a smooth appointment. While an agent is busy with other activities like meeting with clients and others, these presentations are researched and prepared by a personal assistant.

Answering and returning phone calls is another major role for a personal assistant. REALTORS not only have to serve their clients, but also potential clients and other REALTORS. While real estate agents are busy with clients, in a meeting, or performing a presentation, they are not always able to take calls during these moments. When general inquiry calls come in, assistants help REALTORS to stay in control of their business. Assistants are equipped to return a potential customer's call and provide them with the right information they seek. Skilled assistants are tough to come by, especially the kind who know the ins and outs of the real estate world. I know a young millennial man who recently started a company where he trains virtual assistants to specifically cater to REALTORS and wholesalers. Most of these assistants are from the Philippines. I also know of a similar virtual assistant company out of Jamaica. There's a good demand for these types of companies; however, the assistants need to be talented and hardworking, or they are quickly replaced. A missed call is a missed opportunity for REALTORS. This is why virtual and personal assistants are a critical component for a REALTOR'S success and growth.

The Transaction Coordinator could also work the assistant role at times too.

Typically, when the REALTOR goes on an appointment and comes back with a signed listing agreement; the assistant or transaction coordinator is responsible for entering the listing for the MLS system. The MLS (multiple listing service) is the organization that gives REALTORS rules, regulations and establishes cooperation agreements. See, REALTORS work together with a common understanding and join the MLS to share individual listing information about properties for sale with other REALTORS. The assistant or transaction coordinator will have the responsibility of typing out the listing data provided.

The title companies play such an important role for the REALTOR.

One of the last and most important steps in selling a property is the closing of the transaction. Once a buyer and seller have agreed on price, terms; and we've passed inspections and appraisals, it's almost time to close the deal. After a REALTOR gets a signed agreement from the buyer and seller, the transaction coordinator contacts the title company for a search and to coordinate the closings. The search is to make sure the property has no unknown liens that need to be paid off or unpaid taxes. The title company is responsible for calculating any taxes, water bills, and liens that need to be paid at the closing from seller proceeds.

I've explained these roles in detail, not so that you can apply for a job, but for you to understand their duties and see the opportunity to start a business. If you want more insight on starting a business like one of these, schedule a call with me at EmpoweredthroughRealEstate.com.

Thinking of hard workers…if you search the dictionary for the word determined, you might see a picture of Emma Elder-Howell. She's part owner **of Detroit Title and Escrow.**

Emma is a prime example of someone who truly worked her way to the top by being resilient and building relationships. She got into real estate at a very young age, right after high school. Similar to my story, Emma got her foot in the real estate door by working through a temporary agency, Kelly services to be exact. She was a single parent and got a job as an administrative assistant. She started as a part timer in the closing department, filing and making copies for a large construction company. She was very inquisitive and would always ask questions about contracts. They were doing a lot of site condos back then and buyers could get 110% financing easily. 110% means buying a house and receiving $10,000 or so at the closing table. Emma was surprised and thrilled by all the knowledge she was gaining. Eventually, Emma was offered a full time job. The owner of the company owned an apartment complex in an affluent community outside of Detroit; she ended up moving into one of the apartments. This owner also owned a mortgage company. Emma continued to handle closings and later started to process loans. After a few years went by, Emma noticed that she was continuously overlooked for the management positions. She started to

get extremely upset after a newer employee was chosen for the management position over her. Eventually, Emma got a bad attitude, her bitterness was showing, and she was terminated.

Do you think that stopped Emma? Absolutely not! Maybe she just needed a fresh start because she quickly picked up a job at a larger title company. They liked her from the start because of all her knowledge, skills, and especially her background in new construction. Three years later, the same thing happened. She was passed over for a Supervisor position. The company chose an employee who Emma trained and who didn't have half the knowledge Emma had. This time Emma did them a favor and resigned. Emma was so bothered and would often complain about it. She finally felt calm about being passed over the day her mom told her "baby, it's just not your time yet." Emma kept moving forward and was hired at yet a third title company. Now this is where Emma's career took a turn. She started building relationships with the clients and catching problems in advance to make transactions close smoother. The manager and owner of this company had one disagreement too many and low and behold, the owner offered Emma the management position. Ten years had gone by and as the real estate market shifted, her title company got bought out by a larger title company. THE FIRST COMPANY EMMA WORKED AT AND GOT

FIRED. She expressed the department she preferred to work in and her request was not granted. After all that hard work she was told "well Kiddo that's corporate!" She was offered a decent salary of $65,000 but she just couldn't do it. She declined the job.

Throughout those 10 years, Emma had created a real estate consulting company outside of her title company management job. She wasn't sure what she would do with it but needed a company of her own. She knew she didn't want to work corporate because it lacked personal relationships with clients. Their approach sometimes is people are just a file number.

Emma partnered up and started running her own business to the best capacity she could. She sat in a small 500 sq ft. building in downtown Detroit. She didn't know what to expect but knew she was ready for independence. She set a goal to meet the salary she previously turned down. By the end of the year she had exceeded that income and generated $150,000 for her company.

Because of the relationships Emma had created over the years with clients and other title representatives at other companies, she was informed of a title company about to close its doors due to lack of clientele. She was introduced to an attorney who owned a title company. They courted for a month talking numbers, strategies, etc. This company had the infrastructure, and Emma had the clientele. It was a no brainer to collaborate and that's when Emma became part owner and Detroit Title & Escrow was born.

You can contact Emma for title services at eelder@dettitle.com.

What's the secret to Emma's success? Building good relationships, being humble, and staying a solid person with credibility.

What does being empowered through real estate mean to Emma? Being a resource and helping people to grow.

CHAPTER 8

THE SECRET SAUCE

S ome people say "the smartest person doesn't always win in business, but the best marketer does! Marketing is the cream of the crop when it comes to launching and growing a business. If people don't know about your product or service, how can they patronize your business? A great marketer needs to be part of the team for any business. I perform many of the marketing and promotions for my business; and outsource some work to graphic designers and digital ad specialists for my YouTube channel.

So let's talk about social media marketing first. It's one of the most eff effective and efficient ways to advertise these days. The cost can be low to zero, and the impact can be felt almost immediately. *I call it turning posts into dollars*. One example of how social media can be effective without spending one dollar is to "GO LIVE." Facebook, Instagram, YouTube, almost all the social media platforms reward people for going live. Rewards means they will show your post to 50% or more followers and notify them.

Whereas a normal post or pre-recorded video will only be shown to less than 25% of your followers. Another simple strategy that helps bring awareness to your company is to simply post what you're doing. Just talk about your journey in business, or explain details about a new client or milestone. Eventually, you'll get inbox messages asking about your product or service.

Each featured business owner in this book stated that social media is one of the most effective tools for reaching your target audience. People tend to spend more time surfing the internet and social media daily than anything else. The social media strategy is also extremely helpful for REALTORS trying to connect with home buyers and sellers. Most REALTORS use the platforms LinkedIn, Instagram, and Facebook. Few use Twitter, YouTube, Snapchat, and now Tik Tok. These platforms are useful because REALTORS sometimes receive instant feedback with Likes, Comments, and business inquiries sent through private messages. Furthermore, social media marketing for business is a fast way to generate leads, grow a brand, and network with new people.

So let's talk about the Do's and Don'ts of social media marketing and turning posts into dollars.

Do: Be a supporter and liker of other people's posts. If you never interact with others, they are less likely to interact on your posts.

Don't: Be the person always asking and never giving. (Buy my item, donate this, let me sell your house). It can get annoying if you never give back.

Do: Show pictures and videos of what you're doing or creating. Many business owners give credit to social media for making marketing and promotions so easy. They never ask for business, they simply post a picture.

Don't: Nag about people not supporting your business. Many people including family will not immediately show love. However, if you keep working and believe in yourself, after a while, the business will fall in your lap from complete strangers. The universe knows when you're serious and passionate about your business.

Do: Be consistent and post relevant information. Many people make the decision to post two or three times a week about their business.

Don't: Give up if followers start ignoring your posts. Just get better and more creative. Things aren't always what they appear. I've received new business on a few occasions from people who never clicked like on any of my posts; but wanted me to know they had been watching.

When I first started building my real estate business, I didn't have a big budget for marketing. I was simply just trying to use all my money to pay for leads from Zillow. At that time, you actually could get quality leads there. Hundreds and hundreds of dollars went out, but the secret to success is what you say when you get a potential client on the phone. It's a good idea to create and practice a script so that you can convert customers into paying clients. If you are a new REALTOR, have your family role play with you. In the meantime, while I waited for new clients, I would visit neighborhoods and write about them. Or view houses and talk about them. Marketing and branding yourself is everything you do; it's essential for any new business owner.

The key to my success has been marketing hands down. Yes, I put in a lot of hard work like door knocking and cold calling. However, when people get on the computer which many users do to find a real estate agent, I definitely show in search results on Google, YouTube, and most social media platforms users visit frequently. Additionally, reviews from past clients also play a key role for effective marketing. Even if you are a chef or have a restaurant or whatever kind of business it is, sometimes consumers REALLY take notice when others say how great you are. Finally, if online marketing seems like too much work for you; and you'd rather spend time talking to potential clients directly. Many college or high school students work part time posting for small businesses at a reasonable cost. Below, you'll see some of my social media marketing that turned into dollars. I simply posted the graphics below and asked "**which logo do you like best for my new company?"**

A B

I find this type of promotion to be efficient marketing because it really gets attention. People are more interested in your product when you ask them to participate, as opposed to just bragging about your accomplishments.

SOCIAL MEDIA POST #2

My first book 'Next Level Coaching for Real Estate Professionals' was written to help countless real estate agents and beginner investors. I was passionate about sharing my journey in that book because there was a lack of literature, available for new REALTORS. Visit EmpoweredThroughRealEstate.com to gain more information this book. **Now that you've almost made it to**

the end of this book, it's time to reveal my list of the 21 best real estate business ideas.

See below:

1. Bird dog - a person who seeks and finds deals for investors.
2. Wholesaler - a person who finds house deals and sells the contract.
3. Fix and Flipper - a person who buys properties that need improvements to sell top dollar.
4. Property Management - a company that manages properties and tenants.
5. Project Manager - a person that manages renovation or real estate projects.
6. General Contractor - a person that manages sub contractors on renovation projects.
7. Short term rentals - a person who serves as host of something like Airbnb.
8. Adult Foster Care Home - a house for adults that need assistance.
9. Halfway house - a house for people transitioning back into society after serving jail time.
10. Veteran house - a house for veterans with or without disabilities.
11. Real estate marketer - a person who advertises and promotes properties for REALTORS.

12. Virtual assistant - a person who assists REALTORS with online clerical tasks and manages real estate transactions virtually.

13. Transaction Coordinator - a person who manages real estate transactions so REALTORS can help more buyers and sellers.

14. Junk Removal Company - a company that removes and responsibly disposes junk from houses.

15. Cleaning Company - a company that cleans houses post renovations or for short term rentals.

16. Realtor Assistant - a person who assists the REALTOR to help people buy and sell real estate.

17. Photographer - a person who takes professional photos for houses going on the market.

18. Home Inspector - a certified person who inspects all details of the property condition.

19. Package Courier - a person that delivers pre-listing packages and documents to home sellers.

20. Home Staging business - a company that decorates and prepares a home to be more appealing to buyers

21. Home Restoration Specialists - a company that sanitizes or repairs homes after floods or fire damage.

As a REALTOR, each year I realize more and more how essential we are. There are many times we play the role of therapist or friend and at least five of the jobs mentioned above. One of my most enjoyable roles outside of the REALTOR is when I show up as the real estate marketer. Advertising and promotional tasks are second nature for me. You can simply post a picture of a house and say "Just Sold" to get interaction from potential clients. When working in business for yourself, you'll notice that you're always advertising, you just can't help it. Continue reading to learn more about the most effective marketing strategies I use.

» Flyers are a simple but very effective tool for marketing real estate and your brand. Flyers are also used for social media promotions, online marketing, email campaigns, and door knocking. When getting flyers created, detailed descriptions and other useful information are important to highlight; such as neighborhood, agent information, and property history. A well-detailed flyer including several visually appealing photos will easily draw the attention of buyers. On the next page, you will see a simple flyer I used to find buyers. You'll notice it's not asking for business, but it simply gives information to let them know I'm an expert in the field. Below are simple, yet effective flyers that I hand out to REALTORS or in neighborhoods. Online postcards and flyers can be created in just 5 minutes on Canva. Visit CatinaTheBroker.com for discount codes and links to affiliate marketing partners.

Postcards are another effective tool used for promoting businesses. This promotion method works wonders if farming the same area four times a year. Some wholesalers use this strategy alone for lead generation and my good friend in the business has received many flip deals as a result of postcard mailings. Postcards can be a little less competitive because most businesses are not sending expensive pieces of mail too often, unlike emails. Postcards are also seen as open messages since the message it carries is viewed at one glance and requires no extra effort from the potential clients. There are no licenses or certificates needed to create flyers and postcards for REALTORS. But you will need good skills and practice of using Adobe Indesign, Illustrator, and Photoshop. In summary, marketing is the cream of the crop when it comes to launching a business. Without marketing people will not know your business exists. I perform many of my company's marketing myself; and with a little help from graphic designers, ad specialists, and digital marketers. With my YouTube channel, I've cut my advertising spending in half from 2018.

After highlighting all the amazing featured business owners in this book, it's time to learn a little about my start in the real estate business world. I'm Catina, the REALTOR, Broker, Investor, Marketer, Educator, Philanthropist, and storyteller. I write books because I have a creative imagination and love sharing good stories.

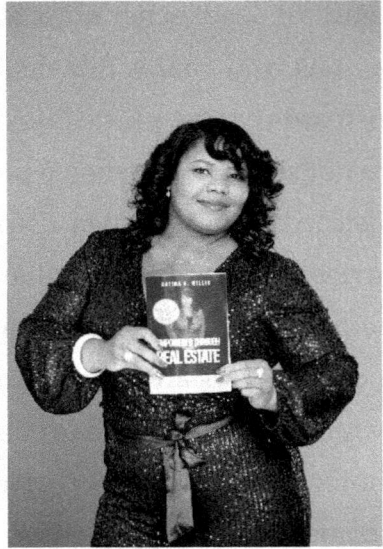

My journey really began in 1993 after the early passing of my mother, Carlene. She died of lymphoma cancer before the age of 41. Things were really hard for me and I felt very alone in this world. My mother was the glue to the family. Always cooking and having barbeques. Once she was gone, I felt like everything that made me comfortable in life was gone too. I moved out of our family home and into a 1 bedroom studio apartment. After some time went by and life insurance money ran out, I realized I needed a skill to get by and pay my rent. I found an organization that was paying people to attend trade school. This was right at the time people were amazed by the Internet. I will never forget the instructor kept saying "The Super Information Highway is coming." This program only lasted about 3 to 6 months but I gained clerical skills that will last a lifetime. I couldn't type a lick day 1 but by the end of the program, I was typing 55 words per minute and 80 words per minute soon after. At first, I went through a few different jobs from temporary services, then one day Manpower called about a data entry typing position. This is how I ended up working at the MLS. I remember working long hours because I enjoyed typing, learning about the houses, and needed the overtime pay. A year later, I was hired as a permanent employee, and 3 years later I bought my first home and first investment property shortly after. After ten years working and supporting REALTORS, I decided to go back to school and obtained a Bachelor of Business Administration degree specializing in Marketing. Shortly after, I was promoted to Marketing Coordinator. Here is where I learned skills that gave me a competitive edge over other REALTORS. During the 15 years I spent working in real estate before obtaining a license, I lost properties during the mortgage crisis just like many others. Thankfully, that experience didn't break me and I was brave enough to invest again. I even teach real estate investing strategies through my nonprofit organization, Next Level Detroit. You can learn more about our real estate investing workshops at NextLevelDetroit. org. Our goal is to acquire housing and resources to support local single mothers dealing with hardships. See picture below of our members and first group of graduates at the workshop.

Mekiele Tovii, Melvin Parker, Yamika Murff, Tiffine Watts, James Powell, Catina Willis, and Dominique Currie (workshop photographer).

Ultimate Empowerment Plan

1. **Love your uniqueness and build on it**. We're all so different and special. Never try to be like someone else. Be yourself by knowing what you like and what you don't like. Your passion will reveal itself.

2. **Take Action**! Once you've discovered your Passion and you have a business idea, go for it! Don't be afraid to do it because others will laugh or others will say it's silly. Remember, I started an Internet marketing company

that everybody completely ignored. Mistakes make us better and help us to realize what we should be doing.

3. **Choose a business name**. Create a name that describes your uniqueness and and describes what your business does. For instance Catina's Cakes or Maw's Property Management. You'll thank me later for this tip as telling what you do will help with search engine optimization once you have a website.

4. **Search business entity names** on your states website. Choose a name nobody else has.

5. **Start an LLC or Corporation**. The form can be printed from the states website or you can file online.

6. **Create a website!** Search godaddy.com or name.com to get a domain name for your business. Try to choose no more than 3 words for your url. This will help people easily remember it.

7. **Get your tax identification number** from IRS.gov.

8. **Get a business phone number**. Inexpensive ways to get a phone number is to use Google Voice. If you're really ready to be professional, try Dialpad, Grasshopper, or RingCentral.

9. **Get a virtual business address** from companies like Regus or Opus.

10. **Open a business bank account**. You'll need to take your Articles of Incorporation and tax id number to the bank.

CATINA R. WILLIS, MBA

Proud to be a child of GOD, a mother, an award-winning REALTOR, and a multi-talented entrepreneur. My love for real estate started in 1997 and my performance and production over the years have demonstrated that I am determined to grow to the top; and uplift others along the way.

Currently, I'm Broker and 100% owner at Next Level Realty &

Investments. In the past, I spent five years at Keller Williams Professionals and proudly served on the Agent Leadership Committee. Since 2013 I've sold over 1,000 properties, residential and commercial as a realtor and investor.

Today, I enjoy mentoring and coaching entrepreneurs about online business strategies, real estate, and business funding. I also love to create educational videos and workshops that help entrepreneurs Level Up in Business. My favorite way of connecting with entrepreneurs and small business owners is through social media platforms and YouTube.

What do others say about me? She's the real deal, she's a wealth of knowledge, and love her energy.

After a successful real estate career and Covid, I realized I had a passion for sharing knowledge with people and communicating it online. The boredom of the stay home order during the beginning of Covid turned me into a Tik Tok fanatic. It really got my creative juices flowing.

Today, I am a full-time online business coach, consultant, and futures day trader. Sharing my real estate, investing, business, and make money online tips through virtual online classes is empowering and refreshing.

To connect with me visit CatinaTheBroker.com.

Over the years, I've been featured on multiple media outlets including: Mlive News, Fox2 Detroit, Detroit Free Press, and WXYZ Detroit ABC 7.

Education and Accomplishments

» Master's degree of Business Administration in Strategic Management

» Bachelor's degree of Business Administration in Marketing

» Four-time KW Maps BOLD Graduate

» Completed Floyd Wickman Master Sales Coaching and received special recognition for Exceptional Productivity

» Dale Carnegie graduate and coach

» Certified Short Sale and Foreclosure specialist

» President and Founder of Next Level Detroit, a nonprofit organization 501c3. Learn more at NextLevelDetroit. org

» Director at Catina The Broker Consulting, helping ordinary people make an income online from home. Visit CatinaTheBroker.com

Thanks again for your support

Dear Reader,

I want to sincerely thank you for reading Empowered through Real Estate. Hopefully this book has been a blessing to you. If you enjoyed this book, please share it on Facebook, Instagram, or your favorite social media channel.

Also, please leave a review of this book on Amazon.com. I promise to thank you or gift you my other book to show appreciation. Let's stay in touch and GOD bless!

Thanks again for reading this book!

Sincerely,

Catina Willis

LET'S WORK TOGETHER!

» To buy or sell real estate, call or text me at (734) 506-0076.

» To start a real estate career or partner with me, call or text (734) 506-0076 or message me on CatinaWillis. com

» To get an instant offer on an unwanted property or project management, email Support@CatinaWillis.com or call (734) 506-0076.

» To start generating business online visit CatinaTheBroker.com.

WRITE GOALS OR THOUGHTS HERE

ACKNOWLEDGEMENTS

Thank you, my direct support team: MAW Investing, Dominique Currie, and Tiffine Watts. I love you and appreciate your support in listening to my ideas while writing, editing, and completing this book.

Thank you to my proofreader Taneal Green and team at Next Level Detroit: Dominique Currie, Yamika Sha'de Murff, Melvin Parker, James Powell, Mekiele Tovii, and Tiffine Watts.

Thanks to:

» All I do is Junk & Quality Cleaning Connection
» Catina The Broker Consulting
» Detroit Title & Escrow
» Dr. Electrical
» Miracle Care
» Next Level Detroit
» Next Level Realty & Investments
» SymRho Investments
» Thompson Business Services

Thank you so much!
Your support and participation meant so much.